THINK LIKE A
BOOKPRENEUR

THINK LIKE A
BOOKPRENEUR

19 Ways to Transform Your Book
into Profitable Products & Services

TIESHENA DAVIS

purposely
created
PUBLISHING

THINK LIKE A BOOKPRENEUR
Published by Purposely Created Publishing Group™

Copyright © 2017 Tieshena Davis

All rights reserved.

DISCLAIMER

This book is intended for informational purposes only. Users of this guide are advised to do their own due diligence when it comes to making business decisions and all information, products, and services that have been provided should be independently verified by your own qualified professionals. By reading this guide, you agree that the author is not responsible for the success or failure of your business decisions relating to any information presented in this book.

Printed in the United States of America

ISBN: 978-1-942838-84-5

Tieshena is available for speaking engagements,
book signings, and workshops.
Send your request to booking@publishyourgift.com

Special discounts are available on bulk quantity purchases by book clubs, associations and special interest groups. For details email: sales@publishyourgift.com or call (888) 949-6228.

For information logon to:
www.PublishYourGift.com

This book is dedicated to my most precious gift,
my daughter, Síva Ann.

Thank you for being my biggest supporter
and motivational driving force.

I love you!

DOWNLOAD YOUR GIFTS!
FREE AUDIO LESSON & STUDY GUIDE

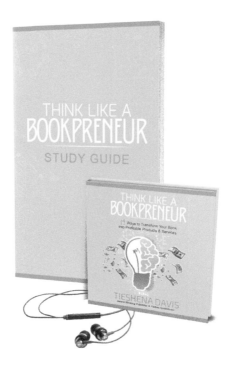

READ THIS FIRST
Thank you for purchasing my book!
As a token of my appreciation, I'd like to give
you the companion tools at NO COST.

DOWNLOAD YOUR GIFTS AT:
www.thinklikeabookpreneur.com/gifts

JOIN THE BOOK PROFIT LAB

The Book Profit Lab is a community for authors to meet other like-minded bookpreneurs who are driven and passionate, and want to become more visible, credible, and profitable!

DON'T WAIT

Join today at:
www.BookProfitLab.com

Contents

Section 3
THE BUSINESS MODEL CANVAS FOR AUTHORS

Section 4
GENERATING NEW MONEY

THIS BOOK WAS MADE POSSIBLE DUE TO THE INSPIRATIONAL PEOPLE WHO HAVE BEEN WITH ME ON THIS JOURNEY SO FAR.

SPECIAL ACKNOWLEDGEMENTS

De'Angelo McCoy
Katrina M. Harrell
Kemya Scott
Precious Bivings
S. Monique Smith
Shani McIlwain
Susan Morrison
Trelani Duncan

THANK YOU FOR YOUR SUPPORT!

Dr. Drai
Jai Stone
Dawniel Winningham
Cheryl Polote-Williamson
Lila Holley
Lamar P. McIntyre
Trinisa M. Pitts

Lynn Smith
Cherise Woodson
Natasha Thorton
Keyna McClinek
Martinae Wills-Watkins
Dr. Oliver T. Reid
La'Ticia Nicole

Tieshena Davis, simply known as Tie, is a prolific writer, multi-bestselling author, and the founder of Purposely Created Publishing Group, an international award-winning publishing firm specializing in author branding and development. She's also the creator of the Indie Author Legacy Awards (IALA), an annual ceremony honoring modern impact-centered writers who serve as unsung heroes within our communities by promoting social awareness, education, and personal transformation.

She appears widely at public events, training entrepreneurs on how to create, package, and monetize their writing to grow their business. Known for her funny, edgy, and direct approach, Tie has become a highly sought-after publisher and a trusted adviser to hundreds of authors through her speaking and consulting.

Recently recognized by Examiner.com as "2015 Best of the Best in Publishing" and honored as one of DC's 100 Metro Phenomenal Women, Tie was selected as a Forbes Coaches Council Member and a Prince George's County Maryland Forty Under 40 Honoree. Her expertise has been featured in *The Huffington Post*, *Black Enterprise*, *Forbes*, *Rolling Out*, *Publishers Weekly*, and other numerous media outlets. With grace, excellence, and a great passion to serve, Tie Davis has become a key influencer to many worldwide.

Meet her and receive free training at
www.AskTieDavis.com

SECTION 1
WELCOME TO THE WORLD OF BOOKPRENEURSHIP

Introduction
So You Published Your Book, Now What?

Congratulations!

You wrote the book, you published the book, and now you're stuck trying to find out what to do next. Like most authors, you're probably thinking about how you can sell books each month to earn extra money, but you don't have a clue where to start besides exploring traditional sales outlets, like bookstores and local events, and promoting on social media. I must be honest with you—that won't do much for you. Here's a brutal fact: According to Book-Scan,

> **"The average U.S. nonfiction book is now selling less than 250 copies per year and less than 2,000 copies over its lifetime."**

These statistics deeply sadden me, and that's the #1 reason why I wrote this book. I'm tired of seeing independent authors fail by not attracting enough customers and inconsistently maximizing their chances to succeed. Perhaps you are too, and if so, *Think Like a Bookpreneur* is for you: the confused or frustrated author who wants to achieve success *beyond* book sales, but doesn't know how.

Why Listen to Me?

Because I get it—as a first-time author, I didn't know what to do either. When I published my first book, *Surviving Shocking Situations*, one thing I was very clear on was my *why*. That alone forced me to think outside of the box and explore other ways to monetize my message. I decided to change my thinking and approach my book more like an entrepreneur would with their most valuable product, and BOOM—it worked. Within the first 15 months of launching my book, I created a thriving international six-figure business. I know, crazy, right? But remember what I said: **I changed my thinking**. Yes, my friend, that's the major key and my intent for this book. I want to help you develop a growth mindset to think like a bookpreneur, not just merely an author. You see, I believe every book has the potential to be the launch pad for a profitable start-up business. You, your book, and your brilliance can make that happen. Here's how I'm going to help you:

The Problem

Generally, independent authors don't publish their books with a huge marketing budget or a team of publishing professionals to support them throughout the various launch stages. Without these resources, they either don't know how, or they simply decide not to properly *plan, position,* and *promote* their books, which results in little to no long-term financial gain.

In working with, training, advising, and surveying thousands of authors who are trying to earn money outside of traditional online bookstores, I've noticed they have a lack of skill and knowledge in three key areas: objectives, strategies, and systems. These challenges exist because most authors omit important processes before and after their book launch, thus making it difficult to tap into their fullest revenue potential.

The Solution

The truth is, inside this book, I do not offer any short-term, get-rich-quick solutions. To address the challenges you face as an author, I will share bite-sized guidance on how to use your book as a launch pad to form a profitable business model for long-term success. I want this book to be the "ah ha" tool that reminds you of the possibilities, opportunities, and advantages of being a brilliant writer! While reading, you'll constantly have tons of "light bulb moments" as you learn:

- The fastest ways to generate money from your book
- How any author can smoothly transition into entrepreneurship
- How to stand out from your competition with your core message
- Non-traditional marketing and sales strategies
- Why author branding is important for platform building
- How to create a simple one-page business plan
- How to quickly increase your visibility and credibility

The Goal
To introduce an innovative model to strategically and systematically montetize your book in various ways.

The Guarantee
When you finish reading this book, I guarantee you'll find at least one "light bulb idea" that you can immediately use to generate a new income stream from your book. If you don't, just send me a note (my contact info is at the end of the book), and I'll buy the book back from you, no questions asked.

Listen, **I want you to win!**

I invite you to take a shot at bookpreneur success. You got this!

Are you ready? Let's get started...

What Is a Bookpreneur?

You might be thinking, "What in the heck is bookpreneurship?" Many would say it's the business side of writing and publishing, such as business formation, legal and tax basics, blogs, promotional plans, event launches, PR campaigns, etc. While all of these "fun parts" are critical, bookpreneurship is more momentous.

At its simplest, a bookpreneur is an author who approaches their book as an entrepreneurial venture. The ideology is marrying the author of a single or series of book(s) with the entrepreneur to become one entity. As a bookpreneur, your goal is to fully leverage your book in multiple ways to consistently make money. To do so, your main book topic becomes the foundation to *build* your brand, *grow* your platform, and *expand* your offerings to generate other revenue streams that ultimately form a profitable business.

Close your eyes and start thinking about all of the different ways you could reach your intended audience with your message. Don't limit your thinking to just selling the book; think on a larger scale. Do you see the possibilities? The benefit of shifting your mindset leads you into creating various products and services that will help you reach this group of people. In publishing, we call them *readers*; in business we call them *leads*. Ultimately, these are the groups you need to engage and serve to transform loyal followers into loyal customers.

How can I use my book to create products and services?

Great question! Each chapter in your book serves as a different sub-topic, and each sub-topic creates different revenue streams. To fully understand and apply this concept, you'll need a business model or "blueprint" to take you from idea to implementation. A *business model canvas* is an essential monetization tool to help guide you through the process of transforming your book into a profitable business. It is the canvas or "blank page" to document your long-term vision and the critical components of market assessment, brand message, offerings, price points, and strategies for connecting with your customers to drive sales for your book and business.

Maybe you're struggling with sales or you just don't know how to get started. You don't know which connections to make or how to gain visibility. Once you design your canvas, these challenges will become less stressful and you will be able to accelerate the trajectory of your bookpreneurship endeavors. Whether you're planning to write a book or if you've already published a book, you'll find that the canvas serves a dual purpose:

1. It will help you outline or restructure your book.

2. It will become your one-page business plan.

THINK ABOUT IT!

What if a person doesn't want to read your entire book, but they want the information that's listed in a specific chapter? Other than the book itself, what mixture of products and services could you offer to sell? Think of the outline of your book as a series of potential products or services.

How Authors Impact the World Around Them

You didn't write a book just to make money, right? If you're like most heart-centered authors, you wrote it because you know you have a lesson, epiphany, experience, knowledge, or expertise that you want to share. Or maybe a particular message that you care about that you truly believe will help make a difference to a certain group of people. But somehow, after the book cover reveal, the *oohs* and *ahhs*, the book launch, and the decline in sales, you've found yourself wondering, "Does my book even matter? How can my book make an impact in the world?" These are key questions to examine before you attempt to transform your book into a business because, practically, businesses are created to serve an unfilled or underserved need, and without knowing what the need is, you'll end up back at square one.

Why does my book matter, and whom does my business serve?

I've asked many authors to tell me why their book matters, but I usually receive a description of their book versus the impact their book intends to have in the marketplace, which are two totally different answers. It's important to get clear now about *why* your book matters because this will also help determine *why* your business matters and further resonate with your ideal customers. Businesses that make the most impact tend to be the most discussed, preferred, and patronized. Answer these questions to assist you with determining your *why*:

- What are you passionate about?
- Who should read the book?

- Why is it important for them to read it?
- How will the book benefit the lives of your readers?
- How does all of this create a solution to an urgent need?

In other words, you want to create your *impact statement*. For example, this book, *Think Like a Bookpreneur*, matters because entrepreneurship has a significant impact in fostering global economic growth and development. Furthermore, it matters because many authors enter the publishing world without knowing how to leverage their books to monetize their message. Lastly, it matters because it is important to you, my reader, because you feel stuck, confused, and frustrated due to low book sales. This book is the solution that will help you develop a thriving business centered on your influential message/topic. In addition to this book, I offer several customizable services to meet your specific needs. *Do you see how this works?*

GRAB THE TOOL:
Impact Statement Worksheet
Download yours at:
www.thinklikeabookpreneur.com/gifts

As we examine how to develop your *impact statement,* understand that this book is no different than yours. The only difference is the very clear *whys*, *intentions*, and *goals* described in the above impact statement. Your impact statement engages your readers and encourages them to become buyers. As you read this book, you'll become super clear and confident in taking a full-throttle leap into bookpreneurship.

THINK ABOUT IT!

Ask yourself: What will the world miss when my business no longer exists? What is my book's impact statement? What will be my business legacy?

determination

purpose

passion

Gotcha
from
Kate

Traits of a Successful Bookpreneur

What does it take to be successful in this space?

Bookpreneurship requires planning, creating, and grow-ing to ensure that your book not only makes an impact but also makes you money.

To be able to do this, you must shift your mindset as an author to focus on treating your book as an actual product and a larger opportunity. If you're not a businessperson, this can seem daunting—after all, you simply want to share your insight, knowledge, and passion with your audience. However, it has become increasingly important in this competitive online culture for authors to understand how to leverage their book beyond simply a few sales.

How do you then begin to shift your thinking from that of a writer or sharer of information to that of an author who also is an entrepreneur? What are the key traits of a successful bookpreneur?

I've discovered there are at least seven key traits that nearly all of my successful clients exhibit. Some clients have more of these traits than others, but each of these traits has proven to support them in long-term success.

Trait #1 – Vision

A visionary by definition is a person who thinks about or plans the future with imagination and wisdom. Hav-ing vision means you can see possibilities of something beyond its current state. For a visionary, everything is a blank canvas; even what seems like chaos can be seen as opportunity for a visionary. For a bookpreneur, your book is that blank canvas. Your willingness to see your book's potential beyond its pages is key to being able to turn your book into a profit-generating machine.

Trait #2 - Passion

Authoring a book requires passion. Passion is the enthusiasm you have for something or someone. It's hard to hold on to passion when, three months into your book launch, your book sales have slumped and no one seems interested. In fact, often you become less interested in your book as a result. But successful bookpreneurs are passionate about their work. They believe in their book long after the initial fanfare and keep the flame burning for the long haul.

Trait #3 - Drive

Envisioning what your book can do for you and for the people who read it tends to evoke passion, which in time fosters your drive. Your drive is your ability, desire, and commitment to push forward with your vision. Passion keeps the spark going, but every successful bookpreneur also must be willing to take action. Drive is activating that passion toward your vision.

Trait #4 - Courage

It takes courage to move forward on an unknown path that many may find lonely and isolating because it is unchartered. It requires taking risks to not only put your dreams on paper but to move forward with them. What if you work extremely hard and possess a great amount of passion and drive, but you still fail? Failure is possible and in some cases, it may be inevitable, but so is success! And so is the possibility that your efforts will lead to unmatched success. As with every entrepreneur, bookpreneurs are willing to take risks.

Trait #5 – Confidence

Confidence, even in the face of possible failure, is a trait I have witnessed in every single successful bookpreneur I've worked with over the years. They believe their book is worthy of attention and they believe the products that will come from their book will impact lives. Having confidence in your vision allows you to see the possibilities of your book beyond its written pages. As we discuss later in part 3, in regard to ways you can leverage your book, the possibilities are endless.

Trait #6 – Persuasion

While the other traits focus more on internal conditions you need to possess, this trait is about how you use all of your other traits externally to turn readers into buyers, clients, and students. Successful bookpreneurs understand how to *talk* to their niche audience. Persuasiveness often comes with practice but is easily obtained through the alignment of the previous traits. Being able to convince your reader that they need your book and its subsequent products or services is key to generating consistent revenue within your new business. People buy when they feel confident in the seller. Your confidence will allow you to choose the most persuasive words. Keep in mind that persuasiveness isn't manipulation. Persuasiveness is the ability

to support someone in understanding how and why your offering is the best, which is the key to all of marketing.

Trait #7 – Perseverance

Resistance, setbacks, and even failures may occur along this journey. A product idea you thought would win over your target audience may fail, or you may discover the target audience of your book has shifted based on current trends or cultural events. At this point, it's important for you as a bookpreneur to remember your *why*, as we discussed earlier in the book. Your *why* coupled with your drive to move toward your vision will fuel your willingness to persevere even in the face of shifts and changes in your journey.

It's key to be flexible, even while holding steadfast to your vision. Being a successful book author and entrepreneur isn't a sprint; it is a journey of endurance, during which each trait often builds off the other, with some traits becoming stronger or more dominant. The key here is to recognize each trait's importance in the success of your new endeavor.

THINK ABOUT IT!

Ask yourself: Which of these traits do I easily identify with? Which are the easiest for me to tap into? Which will require some time and work to develop?

DUMP YOUR THOUGHTS

Building the Go-To Brand

Writing and publishing a book is one of the fastest ways to establishing credibility as a thought leader or expert in your field. Moreover, attaching your name to a book as a contributing author also links you to a brand and allows you to position yourself to attract readers. These readers, when positioned properly, can turn into leads for your business or product. In other words, writing, contributing to, and publishing a book comprise a strong strategy for building a go-to brand for yourself and business.

What is a brand?

According to Entrepreneur.com, branding is defined as *"your promise to your customer. It tells them what they can expect from your products and services, and it differentiates your offering from your competitors'. Your brand is derived from who you are, who you want to be and who people perceive you to be."*

Basically, branding is based on what people think, feel, and say when they encounter your product or service. Your brand is defined by all the consistent components of your business conveyed to your target client or audience. It's the way your target audience knows they have encountered *you*. To support you in becoming the go-to brand for your business or endeavor, it's important for your book's message to be consistent with that of your *solution*.

Making the Emotional Connection

Your go-to brand is defined by the connection you make with your ideal client or audience. When they encounter a common problem, they think of you first as the solution.

Being the solution requires you to understand how to use a combination of visual and emotional cues to connect to your audience through your book and its message.

These visual and emotional cues should trigger what they *think*, *feel*, or *say* when they encounter your brand, business, and book. In the bookpreneur world, we call this *Purpose* (what they think), *Personality* (what they feel), and *Unique Differentiator* (what they say). These are the elements of your book that will ensure you make the emotional connections needed for your ideal audience. Let's examine their definitions:

Purpose - *the reason for which something is done or created or for which something exists.* Your purpose for writing the book is already determined in the beginning stages of writing. You're seeking to solve a problem, bring an issue to light, or share insight into a subject matter that is important to a particular audience. Having a clear purpose connects your intention and vision to those of your readers.

Personality - *a combination of characteristics and qualities that form a distinctive character.* As your book comes together and takes shape, it develops its own personality, which essentially connects to your readers. Think of it like connecting with a new friend: the way that person makes you feel is based on elements of his or her personality that resonate with you. Your book is similar in that respect. The structure of the chapters, the use of quotes, and even the tone of your writing all give your reader a "feel" for you and ultimately the solution you provide. It helps them bond and connect with you on a deeper level, which, for branding, is what makes them choose you.

Unique Differentiator - *a special attribute or value.* Your unique differentiator is how you creatively orchestrate and position your writing and your book differently than others in the marketplace. Purpose and personality will attract or lead you to your audience, but your unique differentiator is what connects you to them and expresses why you, your book, and your other products or services are the right solution and best match for them specifically. It's what sets you apart from any other author, coach, or consultant in your field. When they have a particular need, you become their first choice.

THINK ABOUT IT!

When in the grocery store searching for a last-minute menu item to make your meal spectacular, how do you measure the unique differences between ingredients? What makes one a better solution over others? Now think about what you offer and fill in the blanks:

- My *spectacular* gift or talent is

- I am the only source that people can get
  _____ from in my industry.

3 Key Components to Brand Development

Your book message, along with all the branding components above, should be consistent in offering solutions that speak directly to your ideal audience. Becoming a go-to brand means you understand the tone, voice, image, and angle to position your business. There are three main components to brand development:

1. Identity
2. Brand message
3. Brand promise

These three components, when used consistently and intentionally, allow your book to be the gateway for you to offer more products and services. Let's examine these parts:

Identity - *the fact of being who or what a person or thing is.* Essentially, your identity distinguishes your presence and who you are. What is your book title? What do you stand for? What do you call yourself? What does that look like visually? Your (book or business) identity is the foundation of establishing you as a solution to your ideal audience. Your identity is how you see yourself, your book, and your business, and your reason and purpose for creating them. You convey your identity through the visual elements of your brand, such as color, icon, logo—even down to the fonts you choose and the language you use.

We've all heard the adage "don't judge a book by its cover." However, people often decide what to purchase based on the design and aesthetics of a product. Often, when choosing between what may seem like two equal options, many consumers will choose the "prettier" or more polished option—regardless of its contents. Unfortunately, this leaves most authors at a dead end in book sales and revenue generation. Developing a clear brand identity for your book ensures your book and its contents survive beyond the cover.

While working with my clients, I not only concentrate on creating an attractive book cover or other "pretty" graphic companions, but I focus extensively on cohesively tying all the components of their book into a unified brand identity that speaks to their audience, regardless of whether they've read the book or not.

Brand message - *the underlying value proposition conveyed and language used in your content.* Your brand message is what makes buyers relate to your brand by inspiring them, persuading them, motivating them, and ultimately making them want to buy your product.

The book title, subtitle, cover design, and blurb must smoothly gel together so potential buyers are clear on what they will receive upon purchase. According to book branding expert Kathi Dunn of Dunn + Associates Design, *"customers glance at a front cover for 8 seconds and a back cover for 15 seconds before deciding whether to buy it. That means you only have 23 seconds to really grab their eye and draw them in. Not a ton of time."* Additionally, to minimize confusion, the messaging for all other content, presentations, and related products or services should be consistent throughout the various channels of promotion.

Brand promise - *the expression and delivery of an experience.* It's the statement you make to customers that identifies what they should expect from all interactions with you and your products, services, and company. Your brand promise creates tangible benefits that make your offerings compelling, exciting, and desirable. Consistently keeping your promise is another great way to differentiate yourself, your book, and your business from competing brands and to establish authority in your industry, as you will appear more valuable than others. Remember to keep your word! Otherwise, you will risk getting a bad reputation, which will kill the top two goals of your business: profitability and sustainability!

THINK ABOUT IT!

Ask yourself: What do I stand for and represent? (Answer this question in two to three words.)

Vulnerability
Hope
connection/compassion

CASE STUDY: Lila Holley

Lila Holley is an award-winning, multi-bestselling author, veteran transition coach, and founder of the Camouflaged Sisters Movement.

Challenge:

Originally, Lila had given the book a working title of Duty, Honor & Serve to express a unified message that all military women could relate to. She thought by simply sharing military women's experiences, she'd have a competitive edge, but she didn't know the title alone wasn't distinctive enough to differentiate her book concept from others in the marketplace.

Approach:

I asked Lila to describe words that represented the audience she wanted the book to attract. She used the words: "challenges," "issues," "problems," and "African American." I then asked her, what will African American women share with the audience through their stories? This led her to say two significant keywords: "reveal struggles."

Solution:

Summarizing the keywords, along with focusing on the demographic of black women, created an opportunity to target an untapped market: black women who were (or are) hiding and enduring military struggles. This became the framework for developing a unique concept and concise book title: Camouflaged Sisters: Revealing Struggles of the Black Woman Military Experience. From there, I was able to connect Lila's core message to a visual theme, illustrating and narrating what it means to be in camouflage (hiding), from her perspective. By adjusting the book title and using distinctive book cover elements and a camouflage color scheme, the book made an instant emotional connection with her target audience, which helped her quickly expand her reach and build a new global community for "camouflaged" sisters in arms.

Results:

During pre-sales, Lila and her coauthors collectively sold 680 books. Lila secured seven speaking engagements within four different states and landed six major media opportunities. In April 2016, just five months post release, she launched her own radio show, In Session with the Camouflaged Sisters, which grew to reach 500 listeners within four months. Immediately upon the book's release, Lila was featured on Forbes. com, Killeen Daily Herald Newspaper, KWBU 103.3 FM, The Huffington Post, The Root, and Black Girls Rock Facebook Page.

Testimonial:

"Tieshena is a BEAST! There really is no other way to describe her creativity, tenacity, and marketing strategies when it comes to book writing projects. She fine-tuned my concept and was able to visualize my idea just by my unpolished description of the project. She provides the tools necessary to help authors and their projects remain relevant and to create other projects and platforms to generate income."

Attracting Your Dream Buyers

Remember, your book is not for everyone, everywhere. It is for a specific type of person who is looking for specific information. So while you might think that everyone needs the information you are providing, not everyone will find it necessary to read your book or purchase from your business. Targeting and niching your audience is important in marketing strategy.

Using the example of *emotional wellness*, what kind of person would you target? Are you trying to attract a particular group? Is there a particular ethnic group? Is there a particular age bracket? Is it for Millennials? These are important questions to ask yourself because having a specified target audience makes it easier to relay your message, sell your books, and create other opportunities such as speaking engagements and selling other products.

Though niching your audience like this can seem scary, it is necessary and smart. Would you rather have 100 captivated and specifically targeted people (who are willing to spend money) reading your book and attending your events, or 1,000 people who know very little about your work? With the latter, you would spend more time—and money—trying to narrow down or convince those 1,000 people to buy from you, where in the former, those 100 people have already expressed interest in your work. From a business perspective, you essentially "spend" less money marketing to the targeted audience of 100 than the somewhat random audience of 1,000.

The more focused you are on your key audience, the easier it is for everything else to fall into place, resulting in a well-crafted book that will ensure your success in aligning with readers who have similar values, beliefs, and aspirations.

Your "Ideal Reader/Buyer" Profile

Creating your "Ideal Reader/Buyer" Profile helps you stay consistent in determining who should buy your book and for what reason. Take the time to be proactive in the beginning to identify who will buy or read your book. To determine your ideal buyers, ask yourself the following:

- What are their demographics (age/generation, sex, ethnicity, background, etc.)?
- What are their values and beliefs?
- What books and magazines do they read?
- What movies do they like?
- What online sites/blogs do they frequent?
- What groups do they belong to (online and offline)?
- Who do they follow on social media?
- What hashtags do they use or follow on social media?

CASE STUDY: Shani McIlwain

Shani E. McIlwain is an inspirational speaker and author of the bestselling 90-day devotional, Sharing My Mess.

Challenge:

Like many new authors, Shani tried to promote her book to everyone who she thought would support her. She attempted to drive book sales in various ways but had little results, so her daily efforts became timely, exhausting, and unmotivated.

Approach:

After I reviewed the book, I asked Shani, "What are your core values and beliefs?" Additionally, I asked, "What is the biggest challenge that your ideal readers are currently facing in their life as it relates to their own spiritual belief system?"

Solution:

I gave Shani a marketing plan to include five simple ways to seek out women (and men) who struggle with developing faith and practicing consistent prayer. This would align the focus on a very specific audience and niche market to attract book buyers and secure faith-based speaking opportunities. Vending at Christian-based events, engaging on Twitter, using targeted hashtags, and building relationships were the most instrumental strategies we implemented to help Shani gain more speaking opportunities and increase overall book sales.

Results:

Shani sold 200 books within the first three months of her release and secured three speaking engagements within three different states. In January 2016, she launched her own radio show, Sharing with Shani, which grew to 1,225 global listeners within five months, and she secured a total of 13 speaking engagements by the end of the year, speaking to a collective audience of over 3,000 people.

Testimonial:

"Tieshena is a wealth of information. What makes her stand apart from the rest is that she is not afraid to share her wisdom and knowledge. I love that she gets just as excited for us when we try her advice and it works, as much as she feels our frustration when we use the tools but sometimes don't get an immediate "Yes." She is always available for reassurance and that extra motivation to use just a little more effort."

THINK ABOUT IT!

Think about your favorite brand or the products you purchase consistently. What about them draws you in? Which of their practices or values do you connect with? Why?

Promote the Solution

How do I simplify my message?

Summarizing your book in just a few words or a simple phrase is the most important aspect of niche marketing. The title and subtitle of your book are the key elements used to capture potential readers' attention in a way that draws them not only to your book but also to your brand. Ideally, you should be able to tell others what your book is about in less than 10 descriptive words.

Your book's subtitle is a great opportunity to begin establishing your brand's emotional connection before the reader even purchases or opens your book. The subtitle acts as a mini blurb (short book description) and can be treated as your promotional message or value proposition. For instance, the book title for my client Lamar McIntyre is *Marriage Made Sweet: 7 Ingredients for Making a Happy & Healthy Relationship*. The subtitle succinctly states what the book is about. You can use the blurb on the back of the book to provide a lengthier description and include more in-depth details.

In descending order of importance, list 10 specific keywords that readers might enter into a search engine to find your book:

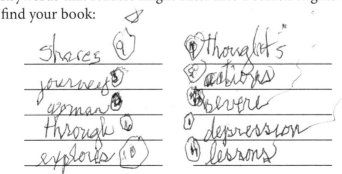

CASE STUDY: Lamar McIntyre

Lamar McIntyre is the author of *Marriage Made Sweet: 7 Ingredients for Making a Happy & Healthy Relationship.*

Challenge:

Initially, Lamar had deemed his book title, The Seven Ingredients to Making a Cake: Marriage Made Sweet, non-negotiable because he didn't understand how niche marketing would impact his book sales.

Approach:

Using a visual analysis, I asked Lamar to imagine walking through a bookstore and seeing a book entitled The Seven Ingredients to Making a Cake with a picture of a wedding cake on the cover. Once he confirmed the visual, I asked him, what did he instantly think the book was about? In that moment Lamar realized why the title and subtitle needed to be changed, so the book wouldn't attract people who wanted to learn how to make a wedding cake, which was far from his intended message.

Solution:

We changed the title to Marriage Made Sweet to reflect the book's subject matter, and then repurposed and revised the subtitle to "7 Ingredients for Making a Happy & Healthy Relationship" to give a clear description of what the book is about. This change simplified his message, making it clear that there are seven fundamental components (or, the seven most important ingredients) to building a happy marriage, which he compares to baking a cake. Because Lamar is a pastor, he easily identified and targeted faith-based events, churches, groups for couples, and other relationship conferences to acquire book sales.

Results:

Lamar sold 50 books during pre-sales and 108 more books within the first month of his official release. Soon after, his article "Intimacy Before Marriage" was featured in the February/March men's edition of Our Wedding Magazine.

Testimonial:

"My overall experience working with Tieshena has been life changing! I have written articles for several magazines, and I am more confident in my writing abilities because of Tieshena, who brings out the best writer in me. Those who work with her will experience nothing but the best. I consider working with Tie a lifelong partnership."

What should I say to promote my book?

Of course, the purpose of promoting your book is to increase awareness and sales, but strategically, promoting a solution for a problem that your target audience may have is more effective. Instead of you saying things like, "Hey, here's my book, buy my book," promote leading and reflective questions around the topic and then offer the book as the solution to the problem.

Tony Roberts says it best: *"Successful people ask better questions, and as a result, they get better answers."* Put yourself in the mind of the buyer—i.e., what are the top five questions that I would ask the author when getting advice on this topic? If you create the promotional questions based on this, your engagement will rapidly increase and trigger sales.

CASE STUDY: Tieshena Davis
& Trinisa Pitts, Coauthor

Tieshena Davis and Trinisa Pitts are the coauthors of the #1 bestselling anthology for women, Surviving Shocking Situations: Finding Courage to Succeed in Spite of Life's Painful Moments.

Challenge:

Developing promotional content that all the coauthors could use to secure pre-sale orders.

Approach:

I merged the key focal points from the book concept and each coauthor chapter title and story topic to formulate five leading questions.

Solution:

I provided all of my coauthors with a list of leading/reflective questions, answers, and various calls to action to use throughout the pre-sales marketing campaign, including some of the following:

Questions

- How do you find the courage to move beyond layers of pain and suffering?
- Are you ready to discover your purpose, voice, or true identity?
- Are you struggling with facing painful tragedies, disappointments, and setbacks?
- Has life broken your heart?
- Are you ready to get you back?

Results:

Collectively, we sold over 700 paperback books during our two-week pre-sales campaign. Within the first four hours of the official release, the book was listed at #1 on Amazon's Spiritual Self-Help Hot New Releases Bestsellers List alongside world-renowned thought leader Deepak Chopra.

Testimonial:

"Making book sales was very easy to do with the questions that Tieshena gave me. Her advice on how to promote the book helped me start conversations with my social media followers, who were just as excited as I was to finally get the book in hand." — Trinisa Pitts

GRAB THE TOOL:
Promotional Questions Checklist
Download yours at:
www.thinklikeabookpreneur.com/gifts

Is there such a thing as giving away too much information when promoting?

Yes, actually there is. I always advise my clients to close with questions. To "close with questions" essentially means ending your promotion with a question that builds anticipation. The idea isn't to grab chunks of content, such as long paragraphs, from your book to share what's inside. This will leave the prospect thinking, "Well, I already know what the book is about; I don't need to read it." Instead, you want to share what the buyer will gain as a result of reading your book. So promoting very short, two- or three-line sentences, quotes, or reviews will be just enough to entice them to want more.

THINK ABOUT IT!

Ask yourself: What are my audience pain points? What keywords should I use when communicating with them? Add these to your promo questions and answers.

Planning for Profit Acceleration

At the end of the day, no matter how much you promote, your efforts can't be measured without knowing your numbers. Too often, authors settle on promoting the book without ever establishing revenue goals or drilling down to identify a strategy for selling books. Why? Because it's easier to get excited about the predictable short-term impact of your book as opposed to examining the unpredictable long-term results. But when thinking like a bookpreneur, this is ass-backwards! Preparing for the long-term results is what gets us motivated and positioned for the unprecedented journey of possibility. Part of this journey is to transform your book into a profitable model that will position you for business acceleration and longevity.

How can I make money fast?

Along with proper branding and marketing, you need a strong sales strategy and a full suite of products and services. Ideally, these products and services are reputable and available internationally. Planning strategic shortcuts on how to produce these items, automate the process, reduce resources, and make more money is the key to growing and scaling your brand. Let's examine the difference between growing and scaling.

Growing is adding revenue while still deducting costs to cover the resources required to support the growth. Although you could be generating more money, you could also be making little to no profit at all.

On the other hand, **scaling** is exponential growth. It involves adding revenue at a rapid rate but only adding costs associated to resources at an incremental rate, resulting in generating higher profit margins at a faster rate.

THINK ABOUT IT!

Ask yourself: What tools do I need to plan and measure my goals versus outcomes? To meet my book sales revenue goal, how many books do I need to sell, and in how many days or months? Start outlining your sales plan now.

SUMMARY: SECTION 1

So far, we've focused on the intangible aspects of bookpreneurship. Many authors, myself included, publish a book because we have a message to share, we want the readers to benefit from content, and we want to make a significant impact on the world in our own super special way.

Every author's dream is to sell thousands of books and simultaneously build their platform to reach the masses with their message. Yet the majority never achieve this goal due to lack of sales skills. Many authors quickly lose confidence when they discover that it requires a bit more than participating at local book signing events or screaming "buy my book" on social media.

Nonetheless, books must be sold in order for your message to be heard, for the impact to occur, and for the transformation to take place. Developing a short, simple, and concise strategic sales plan will get you on the right track to monetizing your message in other expandable ways.

Next up…

Increasing Visibility, Credibility, and Profitability
Due to a highly saturated market, a lot of new authors are overlooked, and while their self-help books contain extremely valuable content, low visibility hinders their sales. This can be fixed by breaking the Authorlocity™ Code.

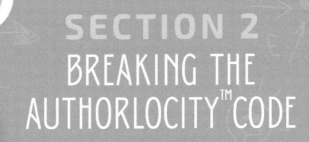

SECTION 2
BREAKING THE
AUTHORLOCITY™ CODE

What Is the Authorlocity™ Code?

The Authorlocity™ Code is a 10-step conversion formula to help authors quickly increase their credibility, visibility, and profitability.

AUTHORLOCITY™ CODE

- Ask for endorsements
- Get sponsorships
- Form your promo team
- Use your online community
- Build relationships
- Schedule bookstore signings
- Leverage your accomplishments
- Gain publicity
- Create your sales pitch
- Setup operating systems

Step #1: Ask for Endorsements

Endorsements have long been the standard in building credibility for your work in various industries. Including a few strong endorsements on the back cover or inside your book is a simple yet powerful way to let your audience know that other people of influence also value your work. Think of the commercials you watch for any product; when you see a celebrated public figure speaking about a product or service, you are more inclined to pay better attention to that item.

The formats in which you receive endorsements for your book can vary. Typically, they are written by a colleague within the same or similar field or a celebrity or public figure who is a fan of your work. They do not need to be long—typically, for a book, they are up to two sentences—but they should be very powerful. Essentially, endorsements sum up what makes your book an important read for a shared audience, so be sure to select individuals who are trusted by your targeted audience. For example, if your book is about women's health, you may want endorsements from female doctors or other experts in that area.

If you can, try to make sure that endorsements are from people with influence, followers, etc. This will help increase your chances of getting more book sales from people outside of your immediate network.

Then there's the most significant endorsement—the foreword—which is an introduction from someone who can lend strategic credibility to the book. This person should meet qualification criteria, to include influence, relevancy, and longevity. Think about it—in the next three years, will a potential reader buy your book simply because a certain person's name is on the cover? How can the endorsement help you achieve a specific goal?

What's the difference between the foreword in the book and the endorsements on the back?

The difference is the length and level of detail of the subject matter. The foreword should be written by someone who can give more insight into the topic and delve deeper into the discussion of why the topic is important, how it's relevant, why you should read it, and how it will help you. Think of the foreword as an extended endorsement that goes beyond the notion of "Oh, this book is great, you should read it."

Major Key

Endorsements

Post endorsements on your Amazon book sales page to improve first impressions and to add instant credibility.

Step #2: Get Sponsorships

Sponsorships are often secret weapons for many successful authors. A sponsorship is when a corporation or business provides the financial backing of an event through
money, goods, or services in exchange for some marketing recognition based on the agreed upon level of "give."
To get a business to sponsor an event surrounding your
book (book launch, book tour, conferences, online event
or webinar, or other events), you would offer the business
access to your shared audience.

   With this type of partnership, you and a business share
an ideal audience. Leveraging this allows you to quickly
raise money or sell more books (and other products), sub-
sequently generating more revenue from the money saved
by having a sponsor financially contribute to your business's endeavor. This can show up as event sponsorships or
book sponsorships (if your topic or cause is of high interest to their shared audience). For the sponsors, they are
motivated by the need to market their business or brand
to your audience. In many ways, your book serves as a key
marketing tool, not only for you but for them. They are not
interested in, nor are they in the business of, writing books
on this topic. You are. However, they know their audience
is reading your book, so they are willing to invest in you.

   In exchange for their marketing or sponsorship fee,
you would negotiate a return for them. It may be displaying their company logo on your marketing materials to
maximize their exposure, a shout out within your book,
or special recognition at your book tour or other events.

Step #3: Form Your Promo Team

A promo team is a group of organic ambassadors who are chosen to help you drive awareness and book sales throughout your promotional campaigns. Typically, they are individuals or supporters of your cause or work; therefore, their motivation is different than a sponsor. They care about your joint audience, but they are mostly connected to your cause or work and want to support it. They don't view themselves as doing you a favor because they wholeheartedly want to serve you in achieving your goal. It's important that the people in your promotional team are supportive, trustworthy, likeable, and dependable. Utilizing this group can be the biggest game changer for increasing your book visibility in a short period of time.

Similar to a sponsor, you share an audience, but it's different in that your promo team does not make a financial investment in your event. Where a sponsor may help you save or reduce costs associated with planning, production, and marketing, your promo team won't make a financial investment but will play a significant role in marketing your book, and in fact, their influence may be even greater.

How? A promo team has the ability to reach individuals within your target audience as they are more than likely a part of this same audience. They speak the language and have direct access, influence, and impact. Your job is to provide your promo team with the marketing tools necessary to convey your message and to sell your books.

While a promo team may not require anything in return, it's best to offer equally valued incentives for their time and effort. Incentives can be free access to your events, gift bags, special recognition, and other perks.

Major Key

Promo Team Perks

Make sure these perks are exclusive to your ambassadors and include special recognitions just like your sponsorship level benefits

Is this only for people who are actively online?

No. For example, maybe your sister would like to assist and she's not connected online, but she might have influence offline. What is she doing offline that gives her access to a group of targeted buyers who she can promote to? Is she connected to community organizations? Is she a part of a book club? What about her nail or hair salon? Does she have children? Maybe she could promote to the faculty at their school. **Always think outside of the box!**

Step #4: Use Your Online Community

Your online community is a wealth of potential. Though not fully comprised of your target audience, it's often the smartest place to begin sifting through to find and craft your target audience. Consider all the social media channels you utilize. Who are these people? What are the characteristics of this demographic? What else are they reading, watching, sharing, tweeting, snapping, live-streaming, etc.? What types of posts do they most commonly respond to? What current events are they most vocal about? Your online community already exists if you have a social media presence. Your social media engagement presents you with an opportunity to further cultivate because you're able to craft a sub-audience from your existing one. Or if your book's subject is for a completely new audience, you can take the same tips to seek out your new audience.

Look at interacting with your online community as casting a large net in a specific sea. Meaning, focus on an area where your target audience is more than likely to "hang out." You can begin to "fish" in that area to identify your target audience. Many social media platforms have easy-to-use tools to help businesses understand who is viewing posts, their habits, and what hashtags they are following for you to track the levels of engagement and conversion.

GRAB THE TOOL:
Online Community Builder
Download yours at:
www.thinklikeabookpreneur.com/gifts

Step #5: Build Relationships

When promoting your book, consider attending events, expos, and conferences. Chances are you'll find fellow authors and members of your target audience in these settings. These events can be expensive, so you don't necessarily have to vend or exhibit, but you can utilize them as opportunities to network.

All networking should be strategic, intentional, timely, and effective (SITE). Beforehand, make a list of the type of people you're looking to connect with, set a goal on the number of people you want to meet, and determine how much time you will spend talking to them in one setting. This networking plan will help keep you focused on connecting with your target audience. Always seek to connect with people who can either become strategic partners, referral partners, bulk sale buyers, or who could introduce you to speaking opportunities.

Networking is all about getting to know the other person—it's not about you. Let the other person talk, and give them enough time to talk about themselves and what they do. If you are just meeting someone and they ask about you first, then fine, go with the flow. But if they haven't asked, "What is it that you do?" that's the first thing you should ask them.

While they're talking, your main objective is to listen for their problem. Start your conversation like this:

- Hello, what's your name?
- How are you?
- Okay great, what is it that you do?
- Ah, that's interesting; tell me more.

Allowing them this time to talk will help classify what type of connection this is. Think, is this somebody who I could link with someone else in my network? Could this be a book buyer, client, referral partner, strategic partner, course student, etc.?

After you've gone through your "qualification ques-tionnaire," say, "Here's my information. Make sure you contact me because I want to talk to you about becoming a referral partner [or whatever it is you want to talk to them about]." Don't just give them the card without giving them a reason to contact you. Sharing the reason creates a sense of urgency about why they need to follow up with you. Make sure to get their information as well, and follow up no later than 48 hours after connecting.

Remember to keep your connection window within 10 minutes because when there is a room full of prospects, every minute counts toward your networking goals.

The key to networking is to view it as the start of a relationship. You may not want to work the room of an event or feel comfortable doing so, but having a plan in place for what you're seeking to gain from the event will guide the types of connections you make. This can mean that in a room of 100 people, you may only need to con-nect with 2 people with whom you can begin to establish a meaningful connection in support of your work.

Networking is about relationships, and the best relationships—the ones that last and grow—are often developed with time, attention, patience, and honesty. At events, you may feel pressure to meet as many people as possible, which typically results in a bunch of mean-ingless business cards and empty promises. When being intentional about why you're attending an event and what you're expecting to receive, you can more easily target key individuals.

Is there a difference between networking and building relationships?

Yes, there's a difference. While necessary, networking can come with drawbacks, such as meeting people who become shallow connections. Building relationships goes beyond networking, and has the potential to transform the trajectory of your brand. One strong relationship can mean the difference between funding your own book tour to having a fully sponsored tour or event. Knowing who to connect with is critical. Relationships can take many different forms and can be developed at different paces. The key is to ensure they are always as organic and natural as possible.

Major Key

Building Relationships

Starting, recapping, and continuing conversations with new connections is the imperative in building relationships.

Step #6: Schedule Bookstore Signings

The purpose of a book launch event is to celebrate your achievement, attract media attention, gain opportunities, and generate sales. A book launch generally happens one to four weeks after the book is officially released for purchase. Whether you sell tickets or hold the event for free is a preference

If you're going to charge attendees to come, the fee should at least include a book, but it's not intended for you to make a profit off of admission. The fee could also help you offset food expenses if you plan on offering the food for free or per plate. It's your choice to make it a private event or public event.

Everything is up to you. There's no right or wrong. But whatever you choose to do, you should have a good flow for the event so you're actually "launching" the book and not just having a "book signing"—there's a difference. To successfully launch, make sure:

- You do a brief meet and greet (take pictures)
- Have someone give the welcome address and introduction
- Perform your reading. It's best to start off with your testimony (your why), then tell the backstory for writing the book (the inspiration), and then move on to the reading. All together, this should be no more than 15 to 20 minutes.
- Offer a Q & A session
- Give acknowledgments
- Sign books
- Take pictures
- Celebrate! (dance, drink, and eat)

Bookstore signings are more about brand positioning opportunities than making sales. As you explore the kind of bookstores in which you'd like to have signings, be strategic and intentional about the exposure you're seeking and how that exposure can bring about other opportunities.

Bookstore signings are a great marketing tool to add credibility to your work and to reach a larger audience. While you may not make many (or any) sales from a bookstore signing, the association with the store or company creates more positioning opportunities for your brand, which is attractive to your target audience.

Step #7: Leverage Your Accomplishments

When it comes to sharing your expertise, bragging has its perks. It is no secret that we are now in a "knowledge" phase in our existence, where knowledge—what we know and how we know it—is more valuable than most tangible things. This presents a perfect opportunity for you to establish yourself as a celebrity in your niche market. To do this, people need to see your accomplishments, i.e., what makes you important or worthy of expert status. Bragging or displaying your awards, bestseller status, media citations, special recognitions, and prominent speaking engagements is your new business card, enhancing your persona and trustworthiness.

Why are "bestseller" statuses so important?

Credibility.

In this age, when everyone is an expert in something and everything can be figured out by simply searching for a video online, credibility is key to targeting your audience. To stand out from the rest, being able to leverage your accomplishments can mean the difference between barely getting $100 for an event and being able to charge

$400 a person for a coaching program. It also can mean the difference between not being paid to speak at an event and being able to command $4,000 per engagement.

Leveraging means taking an accomplishment and creating other opportunities from it with little to no effort. Furthermore, leveraging is the art of positioning your accomplishments in such a way that your target audience is made aware of why you are the obvious choice over a competitor. For authors, it's most important to leverage your bestseller status for joint ventures and speaking gigs, as this distinction gives you a competitive advantage among others. Your status indirectly tells the market, *"I'm highly sought after, and people know, like, and trust me. I offer great value in the marketplace."*

Having the acknowledgment of your audience that you are, indeed, a respected expert in your niche allows you to leverage your book for even more opportunities, catapulting you into new arenas.

Step #8: Gain Publicity

Publicity has a single purpose: to get certain information across to as many people as possible within the shortest time frame. This objective is not to make sales, but to create an image of your brand through an independent source.

You need publicity so that people can be aware of your products and services, their features and benefits, and how they can obtain said products and services. Many authors do not hire a publicist and instead adopt a do-it-yourself approach to publicity. There is no right or wrong way to secure publicity, but there are some considerations that should factor into your publicity campaign.

When you're looking for publicity for your book, you are essentially trying to leverage another company's brand to reach your audience and share your message. This brand could have social media channels or a website, or it could be a mass media outlet. No platform is too big for your message.

There are different ways to get publicity. First, you need to identify the target market for your book. "Everybody" or "all women" are not a target audience. It is almost impossible to market to such a general group of people. This is another reason why it's important to hone in on a focused audience.

Next, position yourself as the expert in solving a particular challenge that your prospective readers face. This way, you market not only your book but also your expertise. Your book may touch on several subtopics, so you can create publicity for each specific topic tied to your book. Select one subtopic and pitch yourself as the authoritative expert on that subject. When you create a pitch based on a single topic, you make it easier for the media to position you within their segments. This can allow you to become a resident expert on a key topic, and as a result, people will want to learn more about you and ultimately buy your book, products, and services.

A complete book can be an exhaustive body of work and too extensive to discuss in one sitting. Whether you are appearing on a Blog Talk Radio program or a national television program, you need to pick a singular focus for your discussion. This will keep the conversation focused on your key message for that particular appearance, as well as give the interviewer a streamlined way to structure the conversation.

For example, if I am creating a publicity campaign

for *Think Like a Bookpreneur*, I may reach out to business podcasts (media) and pitch myself to discuss the Business Model Canvas for Authors, which is part 3 of this book. This is a specific angle within this book, and it is a unique angle that positions me as an expert on entrepreneurship. People who enjoy my podcast interview will then want to buy this book and learn more about my products and services.

When it comes to deciding on topics to pitch, the trick is to pick a unique angle. I could pitch branding, as that is also discussed in the book, but unless the business podcast focuses on branding, then that would be a generic topic, which does not make me stand out. As you look through your book for angles to pitch, think of your audience and what makes you an expert. Consider the unique angle you can offer on your subject matter, which will serve to position you as a fresh perspective in the media.

Step #9: Create Your Sales Pitch

Every author's dream is to sell thousands of books and simultaneously build their platform to reach the masses with their message, yet the majority never achieve this goal due to lack of sales skills. Pitching is always about *sharing the benefit of the offering*. What's in it for the consumer? This notion is also known as WIIF.

The AIDA tool is a great way to craft a persuasive and effective sales pitch. Use the formula below to grab your prospects' attention and lead them to a sale.

A   Attention (powerful headline)

I   Interest (4 *w*s = who, what, where, why)

D   Desire (bullet point the features and benefits)

A   Action (what would you like them to do next, or what's your next action?)

Step #10: Set Up Operating Systems

Being successful in your business is all about being able to replicate your success over and over again. Doing this means being able to set up processes that allow you to be able to quickly create more sales, contacts, and opportunities. Having the right systems in place to support and track your activities (contacts, opportunities, marketing, sales, and achievements) is vital in measuring your success.

Lead Funnel

CONTACTS
OPPORTUNITIES
MARKETING
SALES
ACHIEVEMENTS

These are low-cost operating systems and tools every author should become familiar with:

Amazon S3	cloud hosting and storage account file for large files
Bitly	URL link shortener management
Dragon	speech recognition and transcription software
Canva	creates basic web and print graphic designs
Dropbox	cloud storage application
Evernote	cloud based notebook
Free Conference Call	conference call hosting
Gmail for Business	full suite for contact listing, calendar, and email account
Google Sheets	online collaborative spreadsheet application
HelloSign	web-based electronic signature platform
Hootsuite	social media scheduling and management
InspirePay	online payment aggregator
JotForm	online form builder
LeadPages	landing page for lead generation and ecommerce
MailChimp	e-mail marketing platform
Moonclerk	online payment processor
Selz	ecommerce online store
WordPress	blog and website hosting
Zapier	systems integrating tool
Zoom	video conference hosting and recording tool

GRAB THE TOOL:
Operating Tools Checklist
Download yours at:
www.thinklikeabookpreneur.com/gifts

SUMMARY: SECTION 2

Now that you have learned the 10-step system to break-ing the Authorlocity™ Code, you can immediately begin to increase credibility, visibility, and profitability for your book, your business, and your brand. Taking advantage of these steps and using my insider tips of the trade will au-tomatically propel you into the realm of bookpreneurship to ensure you obtain that **long money** success you desire.

Keep in mind that these steps do not need to be fol-lowed in order or all at once. To start, pick out the few that speak to your strengths and interests the most. Also, never rule out asking others for help when you're unsure in a certain arena. Many of these steps require assistance from your team, community, and business connections, so use this system as an opportunity to further network and expand your brand's imprint.

Next up...

Business Planning

As I have said throughout this book, keeping clear on your *why* will keep you afloat as a bookpreneur and guarantee your success. And just as you need clarity for your inten-tions behind your message, you need just as much clarity in the plan behind your business to be sure you are fo-cused and moving in the right (and profitable) direction. This is where your business model canvas comes in.

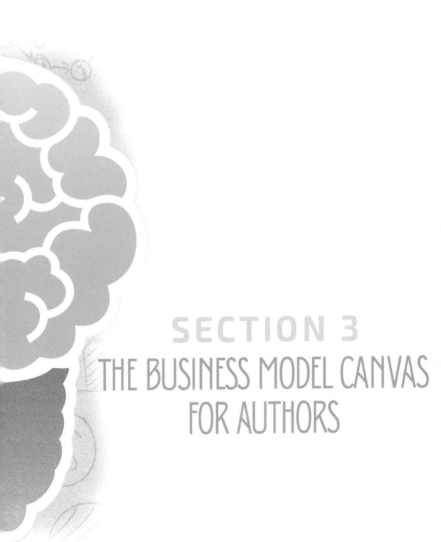

SECTION 3
THE BUSINESS MODEL CANVAS
FOR AUTHORS

What Is a Business Model Canvas?

I briefly discuss this in section 1, but a business model canvas is a simplified one-sheet business plan that details the **nine core areas** of your business. These are the nine components that every business should outline and focus on to meet its overall objectives.

To be clear, I didn't create this concept, but it is a tool that I use for my businesses and VIP clients to build models during the ideation phase for new launches. I've seen so many people get caught up in developing a full-length business plan, which can be very time consuming and confusing to the point where many never execute the plan. Let's examine the components:

THINK LIKE A
BOOKPRENEUR

BUSINESS MODEL CANVAS FOR AUTHORS

KEY PARTNERS	KEY ACTIVITIES	VALUE PROPOSITION	CUSTOMER RELATIONSHIPS	CUSTOMER SEGMENTS
	KEY RESOURCES		TOUCH POINTS	
COST STRUCTURE		REVENUE STREAMS		

#1 Buyer Segmentation

It all starts with understanding who you can assist and what problem you will solve.

- What's the market?
- Who are the people you are creating value for?
- What is the #1 problem?
- What other problems do they have?

#2 Products and Services

Now, think about the **products and services** you can offer them.

- What are the offerings you have?
- What is it that you can get done for them?
- How can you serve them?
- How will they serve you?
- What is the competition?

#3 Touchpoints

Then, start thinking about your **touchpoints**.

- How am I going to reach these people?
- What are my different buyer segments?
- How does each customer segment want to be reached?

#4 Customer Relationships

Map out how you will establish **customer relationships.**

- Is it just a one-time thing?
- Is it ongoing?
- Is it a retentive type service?
- Is it in a group setting?
- Is it in a more intimate, one-on-one setting?
- How will you stay connected?
- How are you working with these people to deliver your value to them?

#5 Value Proposition

Now that you've gathered all of the information on how to identify and serve your customers, it's time to create a **value proposition** (positioning statement) to express that your offering is the best solution.

- Why should customers buy from you?
- How will your offering improve their situation or circumstance?
- What makes your offering so unique?
- Why should they buy from you and not your competitor?
- What is the overall benefit (value)?

#6 Key Resources

Identify all of those **key resources** you'll need to effectively deliver your services or products. Essentially, these will be your human resources and infrastructural assets for your business.

- Do you need a website?
- Do you need a domain?
- Do you need an assistant?
- Do you need a bookkeeper?
- Do you need a manager?
- Do you need an editor?
- Do you need a marketer?

#7 Key Activities

Identify the **key activities** you need to consistently perform to build your business.

- Is it networking?
- Is it vending or showcasing?
- Is it doing joint ventures?
- Is it building strategic partnerships?
- Is it public speaking?
- Is it advertising?

#8 Key Partnerships

Next, think about what **key partnerships** you will need to scale your business.

- Who has access (but aren't your competitors) to the people you're trying to reach?
- Who can you do joint ventures with?
- Who can become your strategic partners?
- Who offers products or services that would be great for co-branding?
- Who can you do quarterly synergy launches with?

#9 Cost Structure

You're almost done! Now that you've outlined everything you have to offer and how it'll be delivered, it's time to start creating your **cost structure** to measure your profit margins.

- What are your direct and indirect costs?
- What's your ideal profit margin percentage?
- How many price points will you have?
- Will you have a low-end, middle, or high-end price point?
- Will you offer a la carte pricing, package pricing, or both?
- What are the pricing tactics?
- What will be your upsell sequence?

SUMMARY: SECTION 3

Completing the business model canvas will help you focus on the core areas of your business so you'll always know what's needed to operate at full capacity. When you have completed your canvas, you will be able to identify:

- Your ideal target audience
- The number one problem your audience is facing
- How your products and services will provide a solution
- Why your customers should buy from you
- The resources and partnerships needed to grow and scale your business
- The most profitable pricing structure

Your business model canvas is not a stagnant document to create and put on the shelf. It is a living, breathing document by which you structure your business activities. All of your efforts to secure and retain healthy, profitable customer and partner relationships should revolve around everything you've identified in this brain-stirring section.

When it's time to scale your business, you can review this initial canvas to chart your journey and identify hits and misses. Utilizing the business model canvas as a planning tool will ensure your business stays on course.

Next up...

Revenue Model

Before we dive into the next section, ask yourself, "For what *value* are my customers really willing to pay?"

Don't forget to get the companion workbook to build your business model.

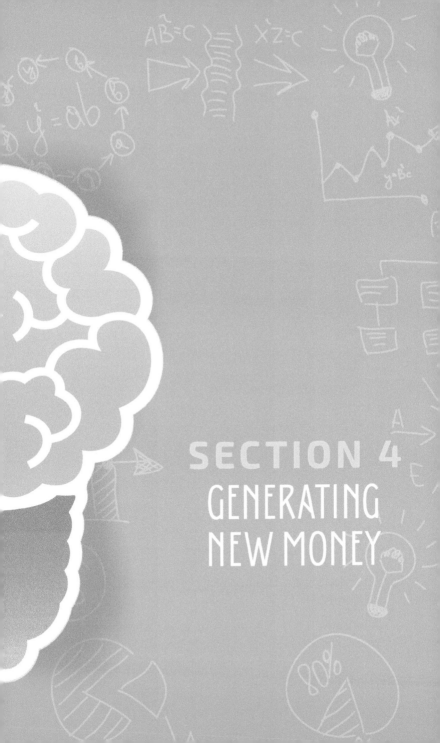

SECTION 4
GENERATING NEW MONEY

Profit Model

Before we dive deep into the ways in which you can transform your book into profitable products and services, let's examine the topic of how to build a profitable business. To do this, it requires identifying the products and services to sell; the pricing structure, bonuses, and upgrades that'll be offered; and a scalable plan for growth.

In its simplest form, a profit model identifies the structured design of your source of income—in other words, how you will make your money.

It is important to figure out how you want to make money before you make it. Once you define a desired stream of revenue, you can then figure out how to reach your desired audience, and the types of products and services you want to offer.

For example, if you're a coach who loves to host live events, live events can be a primary revenue stream for you. Your profit model would include all the ways you can make money hosting live events, such as:

1. Fees and sponsorships secured for your own live events

2. Profit sharing fees and sponsorships secured for hosting live events for others

3. Fees for group coaching programs sold from the stage

It is important to figure out your profit model at the onset of your bookpreneur development stage. This will ensure you have an organized method of increasing your income beyond the initial book sale.

Competitive Matching

In business, it is inevitable that there will always be competitors in your niche. No matter the industry or the audience you desire to attract, there are other books, other competitors, in your space. You will have to design a profit model while consciously diverting dollars from your competitors.

This may seem like a daunting task at first, but it doesn't have to be. Once you identify your competitors, it is time to perform a competitive assessment. While most people will naturally look at everything their competitors are doing, I want you to do the complete opposite: hone in on what they're *not* doing. At a minimum, a competitive assessment should identify:

- Between 5 and 10 competitors in your niche
- Programs that your competitors offer beyond the initial book sale
- Ways each competitor reaches your audience, such as online marketing, social media, ads, event sponsorships, etc.
- How each competitor collects leads for their books, programs, and services

Once you have performed a competitor assessment, patterns may emerge. You may notice that several competitors use the same marketing methods, offer similar programs, and may even use similar branding styles. Here is where your opportunities begin to arise.

As you dive deeper into your assessment, look for those loopholes—areas that they may be ignoring—which will provide you an opportunity to fill in the gaps. A couple of places to find these gaps are:

- Book reviews – Often, readers will do the legwork for you. Their reviews may tell why they love a book, but they will also tell you what the book lacks and what could make the book even better. Cull the gaps found and address them in your offers.

- Social media and blogs – If your competitor has a semi-engaged community, the community may ask questions or make comments about help they need. You can use these questions and comments as insights into what your audience needs. Then use these insights to build your own programs and services, or perhaps include the solutions in your next book.

Revenue Mapping

How do I put my pricing up against my competition? Especially if I'm a beginner?

The math is simple, but developing a competitive pricing strategy can be challenging when you have a unique product or service that hasn't been tested, or if you have little to no direct competition. Do a competitive analysis against similar products or services in the marketplace. For workshops in your area, look at Eventbrite and Eventbee. For journals, Bible studies, or workbooks, go to Amazon.com. To get a baseline on how many products or services you'll need to sell, and at what price point, **always start with the end in mind:**

- Set annual goal: Decide how much you would like your business to gross profit for one year.
- Set your monthly sales: Divide that number by 12.
- Identify which products or services you will sell each month.
- Determine price points for each product and service.
- Calculate how many items or services need to be sold to hit the monthly goal.
- Price, package, promote, and sell!

It's time to build your profitable revenue streams!

Opportunity Alert

Fill Gaps to Create Profitable Solutions!

- Identify gap.
- Create the solution.
- Package it.
- Price it.
- Promote it.
- People buy it.
- You deliver the promise.

19 Ways to Transform Your Book
into Profitable Products & Services

1. Webinars

Skim through your book and review the various subtopics. How many of them could be turned into a training session? These topics can be offered as multiple paid web-based trainings throughout the year.

These webinars can be broken into 30-, 60-, 90-minute, or two-hour durations, and the price points should be based on both the quantity of time and information delivered. To ensure that you're giving rich and quality trainings, printable materials (handouts) such as checklists, worksheets, or an interactive workbook should be included.

Does this only apply to certain types of books?

This method usually does not work best with fiction or poetry books, but in the nonfiction genre—memoir, self-help, devotional—there are many ways to turn the information into a training format.

For example, one of my clients turned her personal journal entries into a manuscript, which is now a published book. Her book is about her life journey as a young woman living with schizophrenia and bipolar disorder. She can easily turn some of the various phases and lessons on living with a mental illness into multiple webinars.

 WHAT DOES IT LOOK LIKE?

The first thing you'll need to do is create an outline for your webinars. Start by identifying three to four subtopics. In this scenario, the author could list three steps in her journey, and each of the three would serve as a single webinar:

1. Discovery
   - What are the warning signs?
   - How to deal with denial.
   - What are the triggers?

2. Acceptance
   - Maintaining your confidence.
   - Who to talk to.
   - How to positively express your thoughts and emotions.

3. Management
   - How to manage your schizophrenia outside of taking medication.
   - Setting simple life goals.
   - Maintaining a positive attitude.

As you can see, it's pretty simple. Break your information into steps, package it, price it, promote it, and sell it!

2. Live Workshops

Like webinars, workshops are small (typically no more than 30 attendees), time-limited, and intensive training sessions where a group of people gather to learn new concepts, techniques, and skills for a specific subject. However, you can charge more for live workshops than your webinar trainings because workshops have a higher monetary expense. The attendee fee will need to cover not only your preparation, travel, and presentation time, but also the expenses for the venue, tangible training materials, gifts, food, and paper goods (optional). This type of training offers close interaction with other like-minded people. This could also be the opportunity for the participant(s) to present their biggest challenge and quickly get the answer or to gain instant access to your expert "insider secrets," which could be a huge game-changer in their business, creating a higher perceived value and investment.

 ## WHAT DOES IT LOOK LIKE?

You've probably seen me mention these steps a lot, but here it is again. And remember—start with the end in mind.

1. Set a revenue goal.
2. Determine the number of participants you want to train.
3. Divide the revenue goal by the number of participants you want to train.
4. Establish your price point.
5. Decide on the duration of the workshop.
6. Identify a venue.
7. Outline the delivery of your presentation.
8. Research the best registration platform to use.
9. Set up your registration page.
10. Promote it and sell it!

Aside from generating revenue, facilitating your own live workshops will also help you increase visibility and credibility as a professional speaker. By utilizing a popular registration site like Eventbrite.com, EventBee.com, or Meet-Up.com, your brand and event will have a chance to get discovered by a new audience outside of your normal network. Anyone who uses the search engine on these platforms to find events in a specific location and on a specific date will come across your event and possibly register. If they don't attend, they still might take a look at your website or become new followers and fans via social media.

3. Transferrable Services

A key to long-term stability is developing a *scalable* business that has the potential to expand beyond the initial product or service offered. This should be planned early on in the development stages of your business, and can be achieved by creating *transferrable products or services.* Offer a product/service mix that will immediately fulfill the need of the next problem—beyond the initial product or service offered.

You never want your client to complete services with you and then revisit saying, "You helped me with [problem #1], but now I need help with [problem #2]," and you don't have a solution to easily transition them into. To be clear, I'm not saying you should attempt to become a jack of all trades, but I am saying you need to be a *master* in a specific specialty area. Always have a solution available to pitch and sell.

What if their next problem is outside of my area of expertise?

Great question! Refer to your list of key partners who can accommodate your client. You can be compensated either with a revenue share or referral fee. This should be determined beforehand with your strategic partners.

Let's walk through the transition process. Start by anticipating the next problem. Ask yourself: What will be their next challenge? What product or service can I offer to help them?

For example, my clients usually sign on for one of our publishing services, go through the publishing process, and then present another challenge that they need help with. Most of the time, it's marketing or sales, or they want advice for specific issues related to their book goals. Since we've already anticipated their needs, we have a variety of services for them to transition into, or a list of products that they can easily purchase. Being proactive in knowing the problems that our customers will encounter has helped our business rapidly scale and remain profitable.

 WHAT DOES IT LOOK LIKE?

Once your initial services are rendered, present a list of your final recommendations, which will strategically include your transferrable services. Clever, right?

Example:

1. Always have a final call OR send a recorded message to discuss the results of your work and future goals.

2. Make a few suggestions to help them achieve their next steps and future goals. These suggestions should be based on your offerings.

3. Tell them how they'll benefit from the suggested products or services. When done with the call, follow up with a snapshot report listing their next steps, future goals, three AMAZING suggestions on how to attain them, and a final list of your recommendations.

4. Make sure the list of recommendations includes other products or services you can provide. This will notify the customer that they can circle back to you when they are ready to move forward and if challenges occur.

Again, some of their next steps or challenges might be outside of your scope of expertise, but you'll still be able to recommend one of your strategic partners to help, and you'll earn a profit based on your revenue share or referral fee agreement. Great stuff!

4. Book Collaborations

Book collaborations (anthologies) are published collections of works from multiple writers compiled into one book. Typically, an anthology is a collection of fiction or nonfiction short stories, but increasingly, anthologies are becoming a fast-track way for writers to leverage their expertise along with that of others (called contributors or coauthors) to position their brands in the marketplace.

There's tremendous earning power in leading a book

collaboration. As the lead author, you (the visionary) can charge the contributors fees to be included. This will help offset the book production costs for services such as graphic design, editing, and typesetting, book launch expenses, and other related project fees; or offer to share profits from book sales, which would add an additional revenue stream to their business.

 ### WHAT DOES IT LOOK LIKE?

1. Get clear on your *why*. Why are you doing it and what are you expecting out of it? What will you do to meet expectations and accomplish your goal(s)?

2. Create the project concept and identify what kind of stories or information you would like to highlight.

3. Decide how many coauthors you'd like to partner with.

4. Determine if you are paying for the project fees on your own, or if you will split the cost with the coauthors.

5. Outline all fees associated with the coordination, production, distribution, and immediate promotion of the book.

6. Determine your revenue profit goal (if you're splitting the fees with the coauthors and planning to include a markup based on your "established platform value").

7. Calculate the contribution fee:

- If only splitting costs, divide the total costs by the number of desired coauthors.

- If splitting costs with a markup, divide the total costs by the number of desired coauthors.

8. Write the project description details to include the book concept, coauthor benefits, and additional perks (if any).

9. Create a lead page or a landing page on your website to include the details above, along with contribution fees and payment options.

10. Add a link for prospects to submit their contact information, or list the "information call" date, time, and conference call dialing number.

BAM! You're on your way to producing your own anthology.

Book collaborations are one of the fastest ways for writers to publish a full-length book, increase visibility, and generate money—all while paying a minimal fee. It's a win-win for everyone!

5. Teleseminars

A teleseminar is a class, workshop, or lecture delivered over the telephone. Attendees only need a phone to participate from the comfort of their home. You can simply send the registration information, usually a dial-in number and an access code, to your customers. You can also record a teleseminar ahead of time and send the link to your customers.

At first glance, hosting a teleseminar may seem simple in today's age of video and with so many visual conference apps available to use. However, you may be surprised at how technology is a hindrance for a portion of your audience. Some people may not be web savvy, and they do not understand how to join a webinar or how to download the necessary software. When hosting a teleseminar, your attendee is not required to download any apps or software to participate live or listen to the replay.

Also, some people may not be able to sit in front of a computer to watch a webinar, or they may not be able to travel to a live workshop. When you host a teleseminar, your attendees can participate from their desk at work, in their car while commuting, in their kitchen while preparing dinner, or while at the playground with their kids. The possibilities are endless, as they only need a phone to join in. Hosting teleseminars can exponentially increase the number of people who attend your event, simply due to the ease by which they can join the fun.

6. Evergreen Tools

People are always looking for the best information and tools to help them navigate through their challenges and reach their goals. This creates yet another easy stream of revenue for you because you've already collected the information to help solve your own challenges along the way. For a very minimal fee, you could collect, package, and sell various evergreen tools that your audience can use over and over again, for an indefinite period of time.

At this point, your customers have read your book and believe that you know what you're talking about. Trust has been established, so they will follow your recommendations once you mention these items as being "must-haves" to solve their problems. For this book, I knew you would need a collection of templates to help you put all of these strategies into action, so I created a collection of tools that is available both as a downloadable file or physical product. Doesn't this make sense?

WHAT DOES IT LOOK LIKE?

Make a list of the must-have resources that you used to help you successfully plan and execute your goals.

1. Where did you get the information?
2. Did you search online? Did you attend conferences or seminars?
3. Did your checklist help you?
4. Did you have a weekly or monthly planner?
5. Do you have a list of social media hacks?

Take some time to dig deep, and I can assure you that you'll come up with at least 10 templates that can be sold individually or as a packaged item.

7. Advertisement Space

With ways to make money through advertising, the possibilities are endless. Let's start with your book. You know that over the lifetime of its release, many people are going to read it and recommend it to others. This presents a great advertisement opportunity for others who would like to gain more visibility to promote their offerings to your audience. When you get to the end of this book, you'll see a list of business advertisements from my trusted partners who can assist you with everything mentioned in this book.

Brilliant, right? But it doesn't stop with your book. You can also offer advertisement space on your website, online radio show, blog, and even your social media pages. A lot of online publications such as the *New York Times* and the *Huffington Post* have customers paying for ad space on their websites. Also, don't forget the major radio stations that constantly share paid promotions. You can too!

 WHAT DOES IT LOOK LIKE?

Identify a list of businesses, coaches, consultants, organizations, or associations that need access to your targeted audience. Then, determine the following for your advertisement(s):

1. Determine either the space sizes (graphic dimensions) or the allotted time (seconds or minutes).

2. Determine the frequency. Is it one time, daily, weekly, monthly, or annually?

3. When or where will it be shown or announced?

a. If it's in your book, is it in the front, middle, or back section?

b. If on your radio show, is it in the beginning, middle, or end of the segment?

c. If on your website, is it on the landing page, contact page, or other highly visited pages? Is it at the top or bottom of the page?

4. Create the price points for each placement, starting with highest price to highest visibility, down to lowest price to lowest visibility. Is it a one-time fee or based on the frequency?

Be strategic! Don't offer this opportunity to anyone under the sun, but only to those who can become long-time strategic partners who will constantly recycle buyers to your products or services.

Advertisement space is always a great way for you to increase your visibility. Use the same list to seek ad space opportunities for your book. Send them an email or contact them by phone with this script:

Major Key

Advertisement Scouting Script

Hello! I'm compiling a list of the online resources that have access to the target audience for my book (fill in the blank), and I'd love to advertise on your website (blog, podcast, radio show). Are you open to discussing this opportunity?

8. eLearning Courses

Unlike webinars that summarize and give a quick overview of one main topic in a condensed amount of time, eLearning courses provide more interactive step-by-step guidance over a longer duration, and can be completed at your own pace. These online courses are generally four to eight weeks or longer, depending on the depth of the content.

Offering a free one-hour webinar can be a lead magnet to attract and compile those interested in learning more. Make sure your webinar and eLearning course both have a catchy title with rich keywords that clearly describe the objectives and expected results upon completion. On the webinar, give your audience enough information so it's clear to them what can be done and what the results will be. This will trigger them to want to know, "How can I do it?" Welp, they need to pay you for that, and this is where you should introduce your eLearning course.

 WHAT DOES IT LOOK LIKE?

1. Think about the most frequently asked question you get from buyers, clients, or customers. The answer should be the topic and title of your online course.

2. Create a list of 8 to 12 steps to achieve the result to the challenge. This will be your course outline.

3. Decide what's needed for each step. Will it be a video, a template, reading materials, a combination, or all?

4. Identify the resources needed to help develop the course materials. Do you need a video editor, virtual assistant, or formatting and layout designer?

5. What platform will you use to host and sell the course from? Will it be Udemy, Teachable, Thinktific, Zoom, or an online portal via your website?

6. Calculate the cost-associated processing fees for each sale to determine your course fee.

There are different ways to sell your course, and many platforms are available to support you with traction, but you must ensure that your content is top notch! This will most likely be your highest priced product, and you want the reviews and recommendations to be 5 stars every time someone completes the course. Just selling one course a day at $297 can generate over $100,000 a year. Yes! What are you waiting for?

9. Co-Branding

Co-branding is a special strategic partnership where two brands join forces to produce one product, service, or event. In this case, each brand brings its unique value proposition to serve the same audience, but instead of doing it solo, you do it together. Think about Dr. Pepper–flavored lip gloss from Lip Smackers, or Pillsbury Chocolate Chip Cookies with Hershey's Mini Kisses. These are all big brands that merged their products to give the customers the "best of both worlds" through one touchpoint and one experience.

Authors can use this same strategy to increase brand

awareness, credibility, and long-term sales. For example, if you have a book about parenting, you could partner with a relationship author or coach to help each other meet specific goals and objectives for a time-limited duration. Again, the key part of co-branding is being able to highlight each other's best features—e.g., you specialize in parenting and the other brand specializes in marital relationships. Together, you're giving your audience the best advice, activities, and solutions on how to strengthen families. Ah ha! Yes, there are tons of ways to co-brand—as always, just think outside of the box.

10. Special Reports

The content of your book can be repurposed in several forms. One of those forms is a special report, a 10- to 20-page document used to generate leads. The report presents a common problem in your niche market, along with three to five of your best solutions, and credentials to present you as the expert, leading people to buy your products or services. Depending on the type of book you have, you can dissect one or more chapters and create a special report. You can take the chapter as is, add an introduction and conclusion, repackage it, and sell it as a special report, which you can also use as a lead magnet to a related product or service that you offer.

For example, this book could be repurposed as several special reports. I could dissect part 3 of this book, extract five of the ways to transform your book, and use it as a lead-generating tool. I could offer this special report at a discount and use it to generate leads for my bookpreneur school.

A great example of this comes from Author Chat Show host Lynda Brown. She has published multiple fiction and nonfiction books, yet she created a special report for authors who want to get their books turned into a movie. She sent out this blurb in an email to her list and joint venture partners:

> *"WOW... I just received some important information for authors who believe their books would make great movies! I've created a 'special report' for authors that will list the website that movie producers and directors use to find new content. The cost of this special report is $20... if you have any authors interested in purchasing a copy, please have them email me at ___."*

Don't forget to get the companion workbook to build your business model.

11. Merchandising

Merchandising is a great way to market your writing, show your creativity, and gain massive brand exposure. Both you and your buyers become a walking billboard, sharing your message without ever speaking a word. Merchandising is also another medium that can be used to further connect with your readers and fans. Adding your book title, personal quotes, slogans, affirmations, and visual graphics to merchandise not only attracts new buyers, but can accelerate your sales maximization online and offline.

 ## WHAT DOES IT LOOK LIKE?

Create an assortment of products to diversify your product mix. To do so, you will need to do the following:

1. Choose one slogan that sums up your message in five to seven words.

2. Choose the top three merchandising items that will attract your audience. Options are:

   a. **Apparel:** T-shirt, sweatshirts, or hats

   b. **Electronic Protectors**: eReader, laptop, or cell phone cases and covers

   c. **Decorations:** Poster or framed wall art

   d. **Stationary:** Post-it notes, stickers, notebooks, notepads, or planners

   e. **Accessories:** Tote bags, buttons, or wristbands

   f. **Drinkware:** Mugs, cups, and glasses

3. Select your manufacturer and order fulfillment company (for online sales).

4. Calculate production and shipping fees (cost of goods sold).

5. Set retail price to ensure a favorable net profit margin.

Make sure all of your merchandise visuals are consistent with your book cover, elements, fonts, and messaging to build a strong brand presence. Departing from this can confuse people and affect their decision to buy if they aren't sure it's the author and/or book they're supporting. Again, merchandising is an effective money maker, but it is also an integral component of your long-term marketing strategy.

12. Membership Subscriptions

Membership subscriptions are ideal for your readers who want to stay connected to you and get all of the latest "insider" knowledge that you're privy too. A paid subscription model would give them the access to different information throughout the year. As you're collecting new information, it can be compiled and delivered directly to them on an ongoing basis. Imagine you're at an event selling your book, and everyone loves everything about you and your book. How do you stay connected to them beyond the book sale? Enrolling them into a membership would not only give them an opportunity to stay connected to you but always give them access to your valuable resources.

 WHAT DOES IT LOOK LIKE?

1. Decide what type of content you want to share. Webinars, templates, coaching time, exclusive in-

terviews, eBooks, etc., are all content options that you can add to your subscription package.

2. Will there be a member forum? If so, where will it be held? You can use something simple like a private Facebook group, or you can build a forum on your membership website.

3. What are the access levels? You may decide on one membership level for all participants, or you may offer different levels and packages to choose from.

4. Give access to exclusive videos and content. You don't want your membership program to contain content readily found elsewhere for free. You may provide exclusive content, such as videos or interviews, with guests to justify the membership fee and enhance the quality of information provided.

5. What's the payment frequency? It is a one-time enrollment, or a bi-monthly, monthly, bi-annual, or annual fee? Be sure to consider the logistics and back-end effort needed to manage the payment options.

Additional considerations may include options to upgrade or downgrade levels at any time. Many membership sites allow you to make a profile that becomes public within the membership community. This provides members the option to use their membership like a network, which is an added benefit. Once you build a solid reputation, a membership subscription program can provide a direct line to your customer base while generating recurring income.

13. Interactive Content

The information in your book will more than likely be amazing. Your readers will have 100 ideas running through their minds as they are reading your content, but they may not have anything to write them down on. They need a documentation tool as a companion to the book, and this is what we call interactive content. These are books with lines where readers can capture their thoughts. With interactive content, you can easily maximize an upsell: instead of selling only your primary book for $15, you can sell two books for $25 or more.

Think about it—it would be nice to have an additional tool to actually document the work being done after reading your exercises and suggestions. For example, a book discussing spiritual transformation could have a study guide companion to document the process, reflections, and next steps.

 WHAT DOES IT LOOK LIKE?

1. What type of interactive book will you add: a journal, a diary, a workbook, or a cookbook?

2. Will it only have blank lines, or will it include charts, tables, or activities to complete?

3. What's the binding type? Perfect bound, saddle stitched, or spiral?

4. What is a reasonable or marketable price?

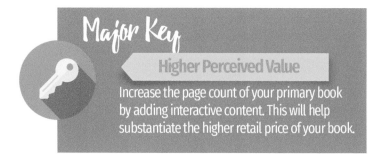

14. Audio Course

Audio can be simple and is easy to consume. If you're using a few of the transformative ideas already shared, you probably have content at your fingertips. Creating an audio course with a companion DVD will give you a tangible product to sell from the stage.

For example, if you're doing live workshops, you can record them and sell the DVD. Then, you can sell the DVD on your website or at your next speaking engagement. Even though people may take notes while you're speaking, there is nothing like having the actual recording to refer to.

I previously mentioned special reports as a way to transform your book. Just as we can dissect chapters of your book and repackage them as special reports, we can repurpose chapters of your book as an audio course. There may be people who do not want to read this entire book, but they want to know specific ways to transform their book into different streams of revenue. Those are the people who will want to take an audio course or buy a DVD of me speaking about revenue streams.

If you have a signature talk or a training workshop, you may be able to repackage your content into multiple audios. Each segment of your training can be its own DVD. You may have people who want specific information in a segment as opposed to the entire presentation. If you record your entire presentation, you can break it up based on targeted content.

15. Group Coaching

Opposed to spending 40 hours per month to coach 10 people on the same topic, why not coach those same 10 people but in 4 hours and make the same amount of money in less time? Group coaching can be done in several different ways: over the phone, through video conferences, or through social media platforms like Facebook or LinkedIn groups. One of the greatest benefits besides saving you a ton of time is the environment it creates for your clients. They instantly join a network of other like-minded people who they can mastermind with to help achieve their individual goals. Once you decide the duration for the coaching program and how you want to deliver the training/coaching, it's just a matter of organizing all of the moving pieces to make it happen.

16. One-on-One Sessions

You're the expert. People are always seeking you out for your insight, advice, and recommendations, and they want to work with you closely in a more intimate setting. It's clear that they recognize you as a valuable asset, and they know you can help catapult their growth. Just as qualified physicians get paid to examine, assess, diagnose, document, and make recommendations, so can you for your knowledge, time, and advice.

 ## WHAT DOES IT LOOK LIKE?

They have the questions and you have the answers. How can you deliver what they need in multiple ways?

1. What's your ideal pay for a full eight-hour work-day?

2. Divide that number by eight to determine your hourly rate.

3. How will you offer your sessions? Will they be two-hour, half-day, or full-day sessions?

4. Will you have rates for smaller consultations by the minute? Half hour or full hour?

5. What information do you need ahead of time to prepare for the session? A list of questions, re-ports, something else?

17. Bulk Sales

Traditionally, authors create marketing plans to target general buyers such as bookstores, online retailers, and book clubs. However, many overlook non-bookstore buy-ers—also known as special markets—such as gift shops, corporations, associations, schools, and the military. These "special buyers" present a lucrative opportunity to sell your books in bulk, on a nonreturnable basis. Similar to licensing, bulk sales focus on using your content to help the buyer meet a specific objective.

Knowing your buyers' challenges (pain points) gives you an advantage to package, price, and position your book as a marketing tool that companies can immediately benefit from. Brian Jud, a leading expert in special sales to non-bookstore markets, says, "Once you change your marketing focus from 'me' to 'them,' you will go a long way to increasing your sales, revenue, and profits." Indeed, this sales strategy requires much more research and creative application than the usual sale, but the return will be far greater than what you've ever imagined for your book.

It starts with thinking outside of the box and applying the simple rule of "doing more with less."

Think about it—you can maximize your profits much faster if you sell 50 books for $10 to 1 special sales buyer and generate a $500 sale, opposed to selling 1 book to 50 individual buyers. Right? So begin brainstorming on how the special buyers listed above might use your book as a marketing tool:

- Could it be a special gift to their consumers?
- Could it be offered as a premium item along with one of their products or services?
- Could it be offered as an incentive?

This creates yet another shift as you begin to think like a bookpreneur. If this was a service or a product, would you just try to sell it to one person or does it make more sense to sell it to a group of people all at one time?

WHAT DOES IT LOOK LIKE?

1. Develop a topic (entrepreneurship).

2. Create a title that communicates solving a problem (Title example: *How to Start a Business with Less than $1,000*).

3. Identify your buyer (Where are the people who are looking for this information: schools, government agencies, organizations, corporations, event host/esses?).

4. Find out your buyer's mission or objective.

5. Present your book as a long-term solution to support your buyers' audience.

By now, you should know the drill when it comes to identifying your buyers. It's the same for the special market: identify what their problems are. What are some of the objectives that they are trying to reach? What are some of their goals? Once you understand this, you can craft your pitch to tell them how your book could help solve that problem.

18. Synergy Launches

In business, a synergy launch is when two companies with different products or services join forces to reach the same audience. They execute the "conquer more together" concept––attracting *more* buyers, saving *more* time, and producing *more* sales in one huge launch, and at an accelerated pace.

One of the most inspired examples of this concept is the 2013 Jay-Z and Samsung partnership. Jay-Z made a deal with Samsung to cross-promote his album with their equally identified target audience. Samsung agreed to purchase one million units of his new album and offered it to their Galaxy III and IV customers as a free download on July 4. This cross-promotion strategy gave the album *instant* platinum status, Jay-Z received a $5 million check, and in exchange, Samsung saved millions of dollars in advertising while increasing revenue due to the demand of customers wanting to hear Jay-Z's latest music. Both the artist and company reached their individual goals.

Authors can use a similar strategy for successful book launches. Mastering the art of producing a definite outcome can be challenging in a saturated market of highly ambitious competitors. Partnering with the right brand can give you access to a bulk of buyers in one large setting. It can also open doors for little-to-no-cost media opportunities.

 WHAT DOES IT LOOK LIKE?

Do the unthinkable and develop a book launch partnership with a well-known brand to achieve your immediate goals. Here are three simple things to do to get you started:

1. Identify three to five brands that share the same message as your book.

2. Make a list of five ways your book will benefit the potential partnership.

3. Create a contact list for all of the decision makers you'll need to reach out to.

19. Content Licensing

Content licensing is an often overlooked strategy for authors to generate ongoing revenue while having a limited marketing budget. Niche market practitioners are constantly looking for valuable information to offer their consumers, establishing credibility, and catapulting their brand. The content in your book is a valuable resource that can be leveraged to help them achieve this goal. Offering your content for usage and distribution to third parties allows you to monetize your expertise and quickly expand your sales channels.

Furthermore, licensing your content initiates an opportunity to develop long-term partnerships with like-minded people who can help you fuel new ideas and conceptual content (and help gain even more sales). Take a moment right now to ask yourself, "What other experts, consultants, coaches, or specialists can I partner with to help them deliver exclusive information to their audience?"

SUMMARY: SECTION 4

Once you have defined your message, identified your offerings, and mastered your business plan and processes, you're ready to get to the good stuff! Using the 19 strategies provided in this section, you will be able to go beyond the traditional sales outlets in which many authors get stuck and take your brand to the next level, opening the door to endless opportunities, connections, and revenue.

It's important to know that there will be some trial and error—and not every solution may be right for your and your audience—but now you have a solid foundation to build on, and to move into the profitable world of bookpreneurship.

Final Thoughts

"Everybody wants to be famous, but nobody wants to do the work" —Kevin Hart

It's time to put in the work!

By now, you may be overdosing on excitement about building a credible brand, increasing your visibility, creating a lucrative business model, and exploring all the ways you can transform your book into profitable products and services to generate **long money**.

Perfect—but remember, being a bookpreneur is no different than being an everyday entrepreneur, with all the highs and lows that accompany the journey. It's intense yet fortifying, just like this book. Growth and comfort don't coexist.

Seriously, I know reading this book was a lot to conceptualize. I intentionally wrote it to take you out of your comfort zone and to stretch your brain to think above and beyond the average perspective on how to make money from your book.

I want you to *think like a bookpreneur*! You have the potential, you have the inspiration, and you have the blueprint; now it's on you to make it happen. **Avoid unnecessary failure** and do what it takes to win. Remember, this is a marathon, not a sprint. Pace yourself. Tackle each activity as best you can, and do not try to accomplish all of this overnight. You don't need to digest or use the concepts all at one time; you can come back later. For now, just take what interests you or speaks to your strengths the most and start there.

DON'T FORGET to join our online community at **www. BookProfitLab.com** to discuss topics or ask questions. Make sure to use the hashtag **#TLABtalk** when posting so your questions can be answered with top priority.

Wishing you much peace, profit, and success,

Tieshena Davis
asktiedavis@thinklikeabookpreneur.com

Expert Resources

Welcome! Here you'll find a list of my trusted partners who are qualified and ready to help you.

Brand Coaching
Jai Stone, Master Brand Coach

JAI**STONE.**

Jai Stone, ULTD
www.JaiStone.com
coachME@jaistone.com
Twitter: @JaiStone

Business Coaching
Aprille Franks-Hunt

coach
speak
&serve™

Coach, Speak & Serve
www.CoachSpeakServe.com
support@coachspeakserve.com
Twitter: @epicaprille

Intellectual Property Protection
Andrea H. Evans, Esq.

The Law Firm of Andrea Hence Evans, LLC
www.EvansIPLaw.com
info@evansiplaw.com
Twitter: @evansiplaw

———— THE LAW FIRM OF ————
ANDREA HENCE EVANS
PATENT • TRADEMARK • COPYRIGHT

Media Coaching
Nurse Alice' Benjamin,
America's Favorite Nurse

MediaRx for Nurses
www.MediaRxForNurses.com
info@MediaRxForNurses.com
Twitter: @MediaRx4Nurses

Monetization Strategy
Dr. Drai

MEDICAL M❁GULS

Medical Moguls
www.MedicalMoguls.com
info@MedicalMoguls.com
Twitter: @MedicalMoguls

Platform Building
Nicole Roberts Jones

fierce
Factor Lab

FIERCE Factor Lab
www.NicoleRobertsJones.com
Info@NicoleRobertsJones.com
Twitter: @NRobertsJones

Sponsorship Consulting
Roberto C. Candelaria

Sponsorship Boot Camp
www.RobertoCandelaria.com
Roberto@RobertoCandelaria.com
Twitter: @RobertoTeaches

Sales Systems
Lamar Tyler

TRAFFIC SALES
& PROFIT

Traffic Sales & Profit
www.TrafficSalesandProfit.com
ltyler@tylernewmedia.com
Twitter: @lamartyler

Website Development
LaShanda Henry

SistaSense
www.WebDesign.SistaSense.com
lhenry@sistasense.com
Twitter: @sistasense

AUTHOR COACHING KIT

The *Think Like a Bookpreneur™* Author Coaching Kit is structured as a portable educational tool, designed to help you turn your book idea into a profitable business. Equipped with practical step-by-step guidance from award-winning publisher and entrepreneur Tieshena Davis, the kit combines everything you need to properly plan and monetize your writing for long-term financial success!

Each 10 x 10 box includes:

- ✓ Autographed Copy of *Think Like a Bookpreneur*
- ✓ The Author's Blueprint to Increasing Your Revenue Workbook
- ✓ Revenue Mapping Workbook
- ✓ Collection of Planning and Marketing Templates
- ✓ 90-Day Platform Building Worksheets
- ✓ The Authorlocity™ Code Poster
- ✓ Quick Tips Card
- ✓ To-Do List Notepad
- ✓ 1 Highlighter
- ✓ 1 Pen

Your Investment: **$~~150~~**

Special Book Pricing: **$120**

www.thinklikeabookpreneur.com

More by Tieshena Davis

BOOKS

Zero-to-Zoom

You Need It, I Got It!

Mommy & Me Diary

Notes to My Daughter

The Mommy & Daughter Cookbook

Surviving Shocking Situations

Think Like a Bookpreneur™ eBook Series

LIVE PRESENTATIONS

Author Domination

Publishing for Profit

Plan, Position & Promote!

Building a Powerhouse Brand

ONLINE COURSES

The Bookpreneur School

Think Like a Bookpreneur™ 7-Day Masterclass

The Easy Book Writing System

Author Domination 7-Day Mini Course

Meet Tieshena online at
www.AskTieDavis.com

Seven
    Good comments on Amazon

    410 - 345 - 5656 (Mike)
         1/8/18
                              .

Authorlocity.
    a 10-step conversion formula → ∠
        credibility, visitability, profitability
Sponsorships
Endorsements → on Amazon.com

/

163

CPSIA information can be obtained
at www.ICGtesting.com
Printed in the USA
LVHW01s1606120717
541028LV00005B/6/P